Living in the Past © 2022 Patricia Leis

All rights reserved.

Presentation by *BookLeaf Publishing*

Web: www.bookleafpub.com

E-mail: info@bookleafpub.com

ISBN: 9789395621021

First edition 2022

Living in the Past

Patricia Leis

BookLeaf Publishing

DEDICATION

To all those who have supported me in my past, present, and future.

ACKNOWLEDGEMENT

I would like to thank my family for encouraging
me to get my works published, my publisher,
and the others who made this selection of stories
and poems possible. I would also like to thank
all the people who purchased my little book. You
are all appreciated beyond measure.

PREFACE

I would first like to start off the book by saying hello, dear reader! Thank you for picking my little book off the shelf amongst all others. Truly an honour, really. I actually can't express how grateful I am. Now, the whole reason why I am here, at this moment, talking to you through the page this way (is this awkward? I don't know), is because my publisher made it a requirement to add a preface. And after googling the word, I was quick to agree that this part was needed. Now, why do we need a preface, or, an introduction from the author? Well, I don't know, however, I thought that this would be a good time to get to know each other. I mean, you're going to know me quite well soon, with you about to read my book and all. So... how are you today? Ah, that's great! Or not great. I guess just choose the response which applies to you. Anyway, enough idle chit chat, I suppose it's time to tell you a bit about the book you're about to read. Well, the ideas came to me over time. It has always been a constant thing with me: I think of some idea that I think is the most brilliant thing since the invention of the spork, and then I sit down for hours on end just transfixed on my writing, and then... never finish it. I suppose it is because I never want a good thing to end, what person does? The cruel plague of not finishing a single story has haunted me for as long as I can remember. Until today! In this book, you will find a rare assortment of poems and short stories which I have actually finished (lucky you)!

Living in the Past is a collection of dark short stories and poems. It is me being quite open about my mental health and how my brain works. It is filled with my poetic commentary on issues which I have overcome, and am still coming to terms with. I see my life as a constant means for self-improvement. I am a perfectionist, and still beat myself up when I do something that's beneath the standards which I have set for myself. I hope that my rare display of openness on a public level can help others to get the help they need, or at least feel like they have someone to relate to.

Even though it was the deadline which gave me the much needed push to complete my writing, I would like you to live with the thought that I did it all for you, dear reader. And, in my own twisted way, I did. I truly hope that you enjoy the little slice of my brain that you are about to delve into. I just hope that you like what you see.

Sincerely,
Patricia

Nostalgia

Yesterday, the clouds wept. Each tear that fell only added to the dampness of the sweeping red sands. The drops leave the only imprints besides those of the wind and the hooves of slow-moving cattle, trudging tirelessly to find shelter. It is the only evidence of life this far out of the township. Thunder rumbles overhead like an old man clearing his hoarse throat. The cattle snort, their long lashes batting dribbling raindrops out of their eyes. They flick their tails to and fro. The stockman cracks his whip and the hooves beat faster. Thick droplets roll over the brim of his beige Akubra hat. The patchy pasture lies ahead, although it is mostly mud now. That will change after this storm. New life will soon replace the old and trodden.

Last week, the sun rose from the east. Its light spread over the ocean's horizon and across the waves like the gates of Heaven opening up. It meets and joins with the white, windswept sand as far as the eye can see. The wild sunflowers are overgrown and block the beach entrance. Patches of long grass sway longingly towards the waves, desperately trying to find a rhythm in the warm sea breeze. Young lads run down early

to chuck the footy. They are soon accompanied
by dog walkers, joggers, and holiday-makers
who wish to watch the sunrise. Surfers use their
boards to plough past the wild weeds at the
beach's entrance, keen for the invigorating first
wave to hit their chest. The coffee van toots its
horn from the car park, its enticing scent
signalling that the morning has begun.

Two months ago, the temperature in the city
dropped. The autumn season started off with
balmy nights, tossing and turning in the sheets.
Even from the top floor of a highrise, the traffic
and sirens can be heard as clear as if one were
on the sidewalk watching them pass. Tradies in
decked-out utes and businessmen in shiny
convertibles clock off at the same time.
Similarly, so do students on their way out of the
buzz of everyday life, a freshly lit cigarette
dangling from fingers that tentatively hang out
of the passenger window. Then, as if out of
nowhere, winter came. It started at sunrise.
Suddenly, the sun no longer seemed like the god
of fire and more like a still presence that emitted
light from above. The air grew crisp and picked
up speed, turning the streets between the
buildings into wind tunnels. Hands shoved in
pockets, collars popped. Cigarettes remain in
mouths; the unwillingness to cause the hands to

even experience a moment in the winter breeze is a strong one. Small children cough in their mother's arms, with said mother wearing a mask to keep her own germs away from the public. But it's to no avail in the thriving hub that is the human zoo.

Eight months ago, the cyclone season hit. Trees were uprooted by only the pure, unbridled power of mother nature's breath. The river extended its banks by several meters, washing up against the sandbags in front of the local businesses; owners at home praying for only minimal water damage, as praying for none would be unreasonable. Rain whipped on windows, shaking shutters. The dogs bark from their hiding place underneath the bed, hesitant to leave their safe haven, yet still determined to try to ward off the beast outside. The supermarkets had sold out of bread two weeks ago. Honey sandwiches, baked beans and bottled water: the only items on the menu for the next week or more. Fears are confirmed when the power shuts off and the township is plunged into darkness. It feels uncomfortably humid and all goes silent except for the sound of the rain patting more softly on the windows. Raindrops form rivulets as they race each other down in a mock Olympics. However, this is only the eye of the storm. Siblings sit in their rooms with their earphones in, as they are aware that there is more to come.

Ten years ago, the neighbourhood kids took a dip in old Henry's dam. The sun beat down, burning and scarring young skin. There is not a single care. This is not a place city folk come to. It's a secret place, built on imagination. Bike riding around the cul de sac until the street lights flicker on, signalling it was time for dinner. This is what childhood should be like. Dreamy nostalgia is broken by the sound of Mrs Henry calling the kids in for a cuppa and a bikky. Lanky limbs scramble up the bank of the dam and race down the paddock towards the house.

Four decades ago, this small country started to filter itself into a more modern era. Cindy Lauper plays on repeat in the next room, the thumping of feet and a triumphant yell indicating that your brother has finally figured out the bold climax to his new dance routine. Sexuality is an alien concept to most in this small town, but with the minority living in relative secrecy in the next room, you do your best to understand. Thick stacks of both old and new issues of the Archie comics pushed up against the wall. Posters of ACDC, Queen, and Bon Jovi hang glorified above the bed respectively. Granny-print sheets smelling of mothballs from sitting in the cupboard for too long. The men sit on the back porch around the pool and drink VB, engaging in a heated argument about the latest cricket scores. The smell of mum's freshly baked fruitcake graces your nostrils as you raise your head off your pillow. You head out to the kitchen and ponder the bliss of suburbia.

Half a century ago, barefoot youths ran home from school through the bush over rough terrain. Their feet, still yet to toughen up, begin to blister and crack. Bloody feet step lightly over sharp rocks and large boulders. Three children, all in a line, scurry around the large ant nest. They are careful not to tread on any of the angry little creatures, who are busy devouring a small animal's carcass. The hot sun beats down on their backs, occasionally shaded when they pass under the branches of brown and withered trees. One youth, a boy, the second oldest of the trio, stops suddenly near a stack of huge boulders. He pulls his report card out of his school sack with a cheeky grin. He places it under one of the boulders and runs to catch up with the others. When they arrive home, report cards are handed out. When the boy fails to produce his, the eldest child dobs him in. Several stern words and

thwacks with the leather belt later, the boy is
sent back to the boulder to retrieve his report
card.

Today, I sit in a small, four-bedroom apartment
in a city in Queensland. The noise from the pub
down the road is deafening, but I sip my tea, fix
my glasses on the bridge of my nose and keep
focused. My earphones are blasting hard rock
music just as an extra measure to keep the
outside world where it belongs: outside. The
rough guitar reminds me of all the times I would
drive on the open country roads at speeds up to
110km/h in my first car. There's no set limit on
dirt roads, and a long skid on the orange dust
looked like giant, winding snake tracks from a
distance. The L plates would always fall off, so
Dad or Pop would have to get out and run back
to retrieve them in the long grass or in a dirty
gutter somewhere. My thoughts come back into
focus as the song on my iPod changes and the
guitar riff starts off slow again, eventually rising
in volume as the singer starts screaming into the
mic. My thoughts turn to static as the shadows
of memories past remain in the background.

Icarus: The Myth Retold

Icarus stands on the cliff face, gazing out at the horizon. The sun has already risen, but the air is still cool with the remaining morning dew. Small clouds spatter themselves across the celeste blue sky. He breathes in deeply, the cool air burning his nostrils. He moves his arms, rustling the feathers of the wings his father built. He flaps his arms, lifting off the ground slightly. He lands back onto the grass, his toes feeling the soft pasture for the last time before he becomes a being of the sky. A god on Earth. With this in mind, he approaches the edge of the cliff, takes a final inhalation and falls forward, surrendering to the sky. He thrusts his arms out to the sides, immediately halting his fall and gliding forward. The ocean spray splashes his face as he dodges the rocks at the base effortlessly. Icarus flaps his arms once, twice, lifting higher above the ocean, but still keeping balance in the breeze. Wind whips in his ears as he soars towards the horizon. Icarus's hands skim along the water as he becomes more confident, dipping and flipping, then soaring higher into the open sky. His father's warning rings in his ears: stay low to the ocean. But what is the harm in flying just a little bit higher? Icarus flaps his arms, lifting him a foot higher. This feels good. The high he is experiencing is unmatched. A bit higher can't hurt. As long as he has enough lift and thrust, he should be able to glide along with the breeze, no worries. With this in mind, nothing stops him from soaring higher, past the fluffy clouds, into the stratosphere, still ever higher. The air gets thinner, the temperature grows colder. The sun above looks so warm, so inviting, like a ball of pure warmth. It's… beautiful. Icarus longs to touch it. Now. This instant gratification should be enough to satisfy him, and then he can heed his father's wishes and go back to flying low through the last leg. He flies higher as his breathing grows shallow, but he pushes on. The air is frigid now, the sky dark. Icarus dares to look behind him, only to find that he isn't looking down at the ocean anymore; he can see the next continent as well. He tries to flap his wings, but finds that they are too stiff from the cold. His bones feel brittle and he is already shivering. He looks back up at the sun as his lungs feel like they are about to give out. Then, Icarus comes to a realisation. Since he can't flap his wings there is no more lift, and without lift, he can no longer retain his height. Suddenly a new sensation overcomes him: fear. He feels himself shift, then slowly, he realises that he is falling. Icarus's vision goes red as he hurtles through the outer atmosphere. He is forced to squint his eyes in pain as the atmospheric heat burns through his retinas and blisters his skin. Melting wax burns his back as he plummets, down, down, down. Burning up with the descent, faster, faster. The sea below approaches closer with each passing second. He lets out a loud, unbridled cry as he plummets into the sea. He hits the water hard, salty liquid immediately flooding into his mouth as he screams. The salt gets into his burnt, cracking, blistering skin; it is agony. His lungs burn, they're on fire as Icarus becomes one with the ocean. His wings are the first to sink, waterlogged feathers pulling him toward the ocean floor. He flails, tumultuous movements trying to keep himself afloat, but to no avail. Icarus lets out one final cry before he is swallowed out of sight beneath the still waves. "Father, I am a fool": his final thought before the surface above finally fades into black.

A Bear Called Suzuki

Greetings! My name is Suzuki. I'm light brown with white socks, and have a bright red bow around my neck, courtesy of my owner, Akira. I've been with Akira for three years now. She adopted me in her first year of university, I don't remember much before then… It was mostly blank memories. However, my memories become clearer when I felt a pair of hands lifting me from my place on the table where I was placed with others like me. I allowed myself to open my eyes as soon as I heard my new name. "Suzuki". It was the first time I was able to really see the world around me, and the first thing I ever saw was my new owner's smiling face beaming at me. Her skin was lightly freckled to match her wild burnt auburn hair, which was chopped at the nape of her neck, and she wore an expression which lit up the whole room. A lad about the same age as her put his hand on her shoulder and asked "are you sure that's the one you want?" I immediately felt my first emotion… was it… hesitation? Jealousy? I couldn't be sure. My new owner just nodded, not even sparing a glance the boy's way and shoved a handful of money into the seller's hand. The boy smiled at my owner and gave her a playful punch on the shoulder. "Well, now that you've got something for you, shall we go have a look at the rest of the stalls?" My owner laughed and returned the gesture. "Always in a rush, Sam!" she mused. I couldn't help but pause to savour the moment. It was the first time I heard her voice properly. It was smooth and commanding, but it had a playfulness about it. I was immediately hooked. I wanted to hear that voice every day.

As the day went on, I found out that her name was Akira. Her companion, Sam, was her childhood friend from out of town. She liked books, drawing and embarrassing her friends in public. We spent the day together as she carried me around in her backpack, pointing out items Sato could buy for his mum back home in the country.

On the way home, Akira had a panic attack on the train. I knew immediately that my new happy-go-lucky owner was not feeling like herself. That theory was immediately confirmed when she rushed out of the train and vomited in a nearby bin. My initial assumptions about her were replaced by concern. I wanted to help her but there was nothing I could do. I felt useless. Yet, Akira held me. I felt her arms wrap around my plump stomach and squeeze tightly as she talked to the train conductor at the station. He called us a taxi, and she seemed to visibly relax. By the time we got back to my new home, Akira looked drained. It appeared that interactions with people, along with large crowds, tired her out. I made a mental note of this. Before we laid down to take a nap, Akira took out her phone and snapped a picture of us together and posted it on her social media. The caption read: "Welcome home, Suzuki!"

That was just the first day of us living together. Akira lived by herself in a small studio apartment in the middle of a bustling city. I'd learned that she was from a country town and she had moved to the city to attend a good university. She had a difficult relationship with her parents, however, she cared for her two younger siblings more than anything. She spent the majority of her time in the city, but always went back home to the country for the summer holidays. That meant that I could have Akira all to myself for the better part of a year.

The next two years rolled by. Before I met Akira, she was grappling with a hefty load of depression. I'd spend most nights with her in her small, dimly lit bathroom, tears streaming down her face. All through this, she held me like her life depended on doing so. For once, I felt useful. We only spent one year in the small apartment before we moved into student accommodation. Akira knew that it was toxic to be alone with her own thoughts for too long, so she moved us into an apartment with three other girls. After this, Akira seemed to thrive. She began looking after herself a lot more, focussing more on her mental and physical health. Life was good, and I was happy to watch my companion thrive.

It is currently the third year of our friendship. Akira has been spending many nights without sleep, choosing instead to focus on her study. It seems to be getting increasingly harder as the university years wear on, and I can tell that Akira is feeling the mental strain. I wish there was something I could do… She scratches her head. Whatever she's reading looks difficult. I can tell she's having a tough time focusing; her eyes keep drifting towards her phone. What could be so important in the outside world that it warrants her attention to drift elsewhere? She knows that she could always come and talk to me, right? I've been there for her through thick and thin! If she's bored, then she knows that I'm here, right? Right? I sigh inwardly. There's no point in dwelling on it since I can't truly do anything about it. My whole life is condemned to watching the life of the person I care about go on by while I just sit and watch. It's hopeless really.

After what seems like hours, Akira finally rolls out her desk chair and removes her glasses, rubbing the bridge of her nose. She exhales and looks over at me with a tired smile. "Time for bed," she mutters. After brushing her teeth and shutting down her computer, Akira lays down in bed next to me. Although, instead of going straight to sleep, she opens the blinds and we stare out at the empty city street. The digital clock beside her bed reads 01:34 am. The moon peeks out from behind a taller building, but its light appears dim compared to the convenience store sign and the street lights below. Akira positions me on the window sill and lays her head upon my lap. She sighs. I can feel her pulse; it's at a slow steady beat, indicating to me that she is content. I smile to myself. Spending time with me is the reason she is so happy. She doesn't need people to be happy. It can just be us, forever...

Akira starts talking absentmindedly to herself. She doesn't realise that I'm listening, and if she does, she must think it's all in her head. She's asking me questions. Do I prefer the city or the country better? Can I see the moon from here? Is it uncomfortable when she cuddles me around my neck? She and I both know that I am unable to answer them, but the silence in the room in space of an answer speaks for itself. She's thinking it too; If I could speak, I'd say only exactly what she wants to hear. "Suzuki…" she mutters quietly. "Thank you for being here for me. You've seen the best and the worst of me. Please never abandon me." Akira… the expression in her voice seems so raw, so vulnerable. I wish that I could wrap my arms around her and tell her that I would never do such a thing, I couldn't possibly abandon her, I lo-

Wait… what was I going to say? My thoughts suddenly expire at that moment when Akira's lips meet my forehead. She smiles sleepily. "Goodnight, Suzuki," she drawls. In no time at all, I hear the sound of her small, quiet snores. Even if these feelings I have are unrequited, I'll keep feeling them until I am a bunch of old fabric and stuffing. Akira's care for me is my only desire that will truly come to fruition, so I shall accept that with a stiff upper lip. So for now, I am content.

Stories of Summer

I originally started writing because I was happy. Today I write only to feel something amidst the sadness. But why skip to the present when the past blossoms more fruit? I remember a happier time. Sticky summer afternoons in the pool in the backyard. Chlorine stinging my eyes, fingers starting to prune after an hour of submergence. Cold watermelon juice running down my forearms, freshly picked mulberries staining my lips and fingertips. The smell of wet dog under the sprinkler as the afternoon drags on. Sunscreen melting off the skin under the splash of water only to leave bright red burns to be covered with cool aloe vera as soon as evening approaches. Stories improvised under the vast starry sky; wondrous tales which included characters like Winnie the Pooh, Piglet, and the horrid Heffalumps. The stretch of the imagination was endless. Stories were written down, typed out and recited for family, friends and strangers. It was a simpler time.

Many sticky summers later, long sleeves are donned to cover fresh tattoos. Legs burn with exertion as the fifth kilometre is reached. Sweat drips down the brow and into the eyes. It is no longer the sting of chlorine which irritates them; instead it is the salty sweat of a midsummer's run. The sun beats down and burns the back of the neck, but is ignored. That evening, under the same waxy moon that watched over me all those summers ago, new worries of the adult world are discussed, shifting childish stories to the sidelines. Imagination is put on hold. Money, relationships and career aspirations are the current themes of storytime. They're not whimsical, or wonderful, or even fantastical; they're realistic. The magic of the imagination has little to no place in the real world, but the stories still live on, however distant.

The Funeral of Eros

Soft grey is the sky, yet it does not threaten rain. It is early morning. The air is crisp and the only sounds that can be heard are the low mumbles of mourners congregating and the bubbling of the stream nearby. The birds do not sing, as it is a day of lamentation; for this is the funeral of Eros. Willow trees over the stream mimic the moods of those attending; stooped over and seemingly weeping. Only one attendee stands alone over the grave. Her tears fail to spill, as the eyes are long past dry. This is not the tale of a lovelorn soul, as this love was requited, but it was only momentary. Years not wasted, but learned from. Time is only relative when it comes to distance, yet that distance was not only physical. Over time, emotions also felt like they were detaching slowly like an old seamstress slowly unpicking threads with her arthritic fingers, the tremors of her hands never once ceasing, making the task all the more tedious. Erotic appetites became unquenchable. The yearning for a release felt unattainable. Adonis, a figure for the next life, feels within reach and yet is, in reality, simply behind a glass wall; unattainable and only for show. Words don't

match up to actions and suddenly no longer
mean anything in this life. The next awaits in its
maturity and wealth. Waiting for a time for
Adonis to take away the soul and whisk it into
the next life feels like the spark is once again lit.
Dressed in black, yet still existing in the same
world as the corpse of desire. Rain falls as
Adonis stands at the edge of the gravesite, hand
outstretched towards the girl. She finds her hand
stretching out to take it, opening like a
sunflower, fingers reaching towards the sun. But
the risk of falling back into the abyss is a real
one. A chasm of this life separates her from the
next, and one wrong movement could have her
falling once again into the blackness, forever
destined to sleep with the corpse beneath the
ground. The temptation to throw herself into the
god's waiting arms and take the risk is a strong
one. However, loyalty remains stronger. The
only choice is for her to turn away, black veil
fluttering in the breeze. Her feet crunch on the
grass as she trudges back to the car, only sparing
a moment to look back to the handsome god,
desire driving her fleeting action. But he is gone.
There is no room for new light here, only old
memories on a stale grave. The corpse beneath
the ground is none the wiser, and this is the way
it must be, if only to keep the peace between this
life and the next. There is no room for novelties;

only few get to taste the fruits of unfaltering
devotion at the funeral of Eros. The rest wander
in darkness. Forever. Until death doest thou part.

Love, As Far As I'm Concerned

To me, love feels unpredictable, yet this is
cushioned by the unconditional nature of it. It
feels like belly laughs, sore cheeks from smiling
and genuine emotions. It feels like the freedom
to be one's self. It feels playful and addictive in
all the right ways, and yet stable and supportive.
Love feels like a blindfolded step off a cliff with
the knowledge that you will be caught at the
bottom. Love, to me, feels safe. It feels like
someone who I know will be a home for me and
a comfort when I am feeling at my most
vulnerable. It is the notion of letting me in, just
as much as I have opened myself up in return.
Love is friendship, love requires effort, and love
is loyal, and love is beautiful.

However, love can be toxic. Love can hurt. Love
can sting and tear you in two and leave you
crying so hard you're heaving for breath. It feels
like you've lost everything. Your world is
shattered, foggy. You feel useless and
abandoned. Desperation engulfs you. This is the
twisted side of love. Lines are crossed and bonds
are broken. True love is shattered, and manic

obsession takes hold. All seven stages of grief are felt at once. You feel like you're breaking from the inside out.

But love can also lift you up. The sunrise on the darkness which clouds the mind, pulling you out of your slump. Love is clarity. Love can destroy, but love can heal. Love is human.

Anamnesis of Poison

Blood on my fingers, toes, stomach… It matters not that facts are facts; it's only my assumptions of myself which dominate emotions. Swirling, burning, feverish. The theory of bliss is only relative until it is proven factual, but what are facts when the world around us is currently determined by bias? Politics mean nothing in this sense of speaking. I only have myself to blame, without explicitly identifying it as "blame". The way words are said, sentences are stringed together, communication is exchanged, all builds to a crescendo. How reactions are perceived, how one regards one's self. It all comes down to silent, biased observation. A one-sided mirror looking out and only the individual can be seen. Raw, imperfect, disturbed. Within the eye of the storm, caged in an internal padded cell, lies the end. It is the depth of the being. Rigid, confined, suffocating. An anger at oneself so rich a substance that if it leaked out it would be priceless. Nothing to see, nothing to do. Just observe, pick at chains, bite at nails, crack my own bones just to feel something, anything other than hate for myself. As one claw's one's way to the surface, gasping for air, it becomes brighter. The sky is cloudy, but the sun shines through every now and again.

Feet pound the pavement, moving faster and faster as the daylight burns into pale flesh, causing it to sear and disfigure. This pain can't end until the mind is satisfied that the body has suffered enough. The inner demon looks on in amusement as the outer body suffers. It whispers its cruel nothings with wicked intent, causing the mind to deteriorate and the vision to blur. The sense of sight is dead in every sense. There is only darkness to wander in now. Blurry, demonic, addictive. Every stage of one's life brings up new struggles which the demon thrives in, and yet the surface, no matter how crippled and exhausted, persists and overcomes. From turning apples into apple juice and swallowing inactive substances. Living, yet not living. But the mind overcame. The body blossomed. The heart healed. Yet the demon perists. Stages flicker past like a film roll switched to accelerate. Blood means nothing; it only exists as a word to add on to. It is the beginning of all, and yet ends at nothing. Heartache, headache, and sickness of the mind pollute the senses and act as peroxide. No matter how thick, blood will always dissolve. Ashes to ashes. Ties are broken within myself. Tear ducts rupture. The throat burns. This breed of pain is far from sweet. Blood on my fingers, toes, and stomach… it stains, and nothing matters.

Insomniac / The Witch Doctor's Apprentice

The young woman awoke in a sweat. It was 3am and the air around her was chilled, yet sticky with humidity. The window to her right had fogged to the point that she couldn't see the stars outside in the cold night. She could see her breath in the moonlight which streamed in through her window, along with city lights; more people who she figured couldn't sleep either. Her back felt icy, although that was due to it being damp along with her sheets. She sighed and sat up, pushing the sodden sheets off her. A musky smell hit her nostrils. She exhaled harshly and made a mental note to push laundry day forward to tomorrow instead of Sunday. Rolling her shoulders back, the young woman slid out of her bed and made her way out to the small hallway which led to her kitchen. The automatic light went on, blinding her momentarily. Her eyes had adjusted to the dark, so the harshness of the light came as a sudden pang to the senses. The only sound that could be heard was the sound of her sock clad feet padding along the linoleum.

The wooden chair squeaked across the floor as she pulled it out from the dining room table and slumped down. Scooting it in so she was comfortably seated at the table, she pulled out her laptop and started it up. The device stirred to life, covering the woman's face in a bright blue light. She sighed, typing in her password and pulling up a word document. Her typing was the only sound that could be heard, along with the woman's soft breaths. Writing soothed her; it was a way she could escape reality. And, in the dead of night, she could focus on escaping with no outside stimulants to impede on her thoughts. Bliss. Tonight, she decided to escape to her fantasy world. She typed:

31st December, 1833

Dear Diary,

I honestly don't know where to start. I am turning sixteen in March. Since this is the first year of my apprenticeship, I want to record every detail (hence why I bought this journal). Today was particularly exciting because I moved out of my parents' house and moved in with my tutor, simply known as The Witch Doctor, or "Doc" as I call him. He's the local healer in London town and he's quite the local celebrity! I still don't know his real name… no one does. At first, I thought that it was rather peculiar when he introduced himself to me a little over a month ago.

I was working on the street, selling matches in exchange for bread money. It was cold that day, and my thin, torn socks were the only things I wore on my feet, so they didn't offer me much protection from the frost. I was shivering, the matches I carried shook and rattled in the small box in my hands. I had been standing there on the corner for hours. People walked past me without a second look as I stood there shaking and pleading for a sale. Before I knew it, the gas lamps were being lit as the street darkened. Black smog mixed with the chilly night air, causing me to cough and splutter; my lungs had always been bad. I didn't hear any footprints approach me, but I noticed a long shadow looming over me. I glanced up and that's when I saw him for the first time. He was a tall, thin man, wearing a white dress shirt under a black suit and tie, donned with a long, black coat. He wore a black wide brim hat and thoroughly polished black shoes. However, the most peculiar thing about him was that he wore a long, beaked mask over his face. I recognised it immediately as the mask which plague doctors wore in the days of old. Since I couldn't see his face, I felt rather fearful. As if sensing this, he knelt down onto one knee in front of me and presented a silver coin to me from his white, gloved hand. He wanted to buy a match? I reached out to take the coin, but before I could take it from him, he placed his other hand on top of mine, so my own hand was sandwiched between his two gloved ones.

"Your cough…" he spoke. His voice was somewhat muffled by the mask, but it was a kind sounding voice. He had a velvety, posh accent, but there was a cockney rhythm in there too, as if he had grown up locally, but had somehow come into money.
"My… cough? What about it?" I asked hesitantly.
"How long have you had it?" He inquired. I stilled. Was he actually a healer? Or was he just some posh weirdo trying to gain my trust? Opting to leave myself open and reluctantly trust the man, I answered. "Since I was very young. Can't remember though." I sniffled; the cold air was starting to get to me. The man suddenly stood up, straightened his coat and looked down at me with his large, beaked mask.
"I have something for that. Would you care to follow me?"

"Um…" I started, but he held out his hand expectantly for me to take it.

"No need to worry, I'm not some creep. I'm The Witch Doctor. You can call me "Doc" if it will make you more comfortable." I could sense a reassuring smile behind his mask. "Now, would you care to accompany me? It is getting quite dark on these streets and a young lady like yourself shouldn't be out here without an escort."

I looked around. Like The Witch Doctor had clearly stated, it had gotten very dark indeed, and also very cold. I coughed again, this time feeling my lungs burn as I breathed in the surrounding smog. That was all the confirmation I needed. I reached out and took Doc's hand.

I was led along the main street, before turning off into a small alleyway between a cobbler's shop and a butcher. The alleyway was dark, the only light to see was streaming in from the street, which slowly dimmed the further we walked. I started to become scared. Was this all a trick? Did Doc lie? Was his name even "Doc"? So many questions flowed through my mind as I thought of my parents. Would they be worried? Or would they be happy that they had one less mouth to feed?

I was too lost in my thoughts to realise that we
had stopped in front of a narrow, wooden door
with a small sign on the front. It was too dark to
see what the sign said, but it looked like the
entrance to a small shop. The Witch Doctor took
out a set of keys and fumbled for the lock in the
darkness for a bit before the door creaked open
and he stepped inside. Hesitantly, I stepped
inside. My lungs were immediately filled with
warm air and the smell of chemicals, and I
started coughing again. The Witch Doctor
crossed to the right side of the room and lit a gas
lamp. In the dim light, I could just make out the
room around me. It looked like a surgery, and
the familiar feeling of uncertainty reared its head
inside me. Small, dusty vials of liquid sat on the
long shelves which lined the far wall. A lengthy,
steel table sat in the centre of the room, and a
little wooden desk was set up beside it. On the
desk, I saw small metal instruments, which I
soon realised were medical tools used for
surgeries. To the far right of the room, was a
larger wooden desk, a large chair sitting behind
it and two smaller wooden chairs facing it on the
opposite side. To the far left corner of the room
sat various potted plants under a large window
which stretched out spanning almost the entire
wall. I had never seen such plants in my life!
Some were orange, others green with red berries,

another was vine-like. Fear melted out of my
body as I stared, transfixed.

The Witch Doctor walked to the far end of the
room and grabbed a small bottle filled with a
clear liquid. "I see you like the licorice plant."
He said, amusement in his voice. I snapped out
of my trance and looked back at him. "Licorice
plant?" I asked. He chuckled.
"Yes. Its root extract is actually what is in this
bottle. I've discovered that it is very good for
ailments of the respiratory system. Would you
like to try it?"
I gulped, hesitant, but my curiosity got the better
of me and I nodded. Doc popped the cork off the
vial and handed it to me. I smelt the liquid inside
and gagged. I looked back up at The Doctor,
who remained expressionless in his mask.
Feeling like I had nothing to lose, I held my nose
and gulped down the contents of the bottle.
Immediately, I felt a warm sensation inside me,
and I didn't feel the need to cough anymore.
What was that stuff? A plant? A plant that cured
my coughing? I looked up to Doc, my eyes
sparkling with curiosity. I wanted to learn more.
Doc chuckled.
"You're a curious one aren't you?" He pondered
for a moment. "I've actually been looking for an
apprentice for a little while now, and you seem

eager to learn. Would you like to learn how to be a healer?"

Without a shred of hesitation, I nodded. Anything was better than selling matches on the street, and this seemed like it would be something I would enjoy learning about. Doc nodded.

"Then it's settled! You'll start at the beginning of the new year. Meet me back here at 4pm on the 1st of January."

And that's how my story begins.

1st January, 1834

Dear Diary,

It was a little difficult to find the place seeing as last time I went there it was pitch blackness, but I managed to find the alleyway nonetheless. I found the familiar wooden door, now lit by the dying streams of daylight. The sign, which I couldn't make out on my previous visit, read "The Witch Doctor. Healer. Please Enter" in official-looking letters which were carved into a wooden plaque which matched the door it was attached to. I knocked tentatively.

"I just realised," he exclaimed, "I never asked for your name! How rude of me!"

I blushed. It was rude of him, but I would've never said it to his face. "It's Sallie. Pleasure working with you sir." I flashed a toothy grin.

***

The young woman rubbed her eyes and stretched back on the dining room chair. Her eyes felt heavy. It felt good to delve into her own version of reality again. "The Witch Doctor's Apprentice" was her newest work, and she was quite proud of it. The story was a reality she could control, and it would write itself on her terms. In her world, she would never lay awake for hours, thinking about the friends she lost and a past she couldn't change. She would never have horrible nightmares unless she herself willed it be. The woman pushed the chair back, closed the laptop, and padded back to bed. She would finish this story on another sleepless night.

Abandonment Issues

I'm largely independent, I have my priorities in
check,
But when I'm in a relationship, I'm an
over-sensitive wreck.
I'm clingy and self-conscious, by fault of a
parent
Who, all throughout my childhood, was
abhorrently errant.
Analysing the mind comes up with no
blankness,
Pieces falling into place as to why I'm so
anxious.
A soul filled with trauma from the past in
fragments,
The shocking realisation that I have skewed
emotional attachments.
Feelings which, overall, are difficult to articulate
When the love addiction I possess wills me to
manipulate.
Stay with me forever, please, don't leave me all
alone,
A conditioned people pleaser; obedience I've
never outgrown.
Childhood wounds splinter the soul, distorting
what's right in front of me,

I try to mask it best I can, but lack emotional
responsibility.
I adjust myself to fit in with others, is this some
kind of disorder?
But self-diagnosis does no good when my brain
already lacks order.
I cling to those on a pedestal, and look to them
to solve my issues,
A toxic dependency I'm slowly mending, with
piles and piles of tissues.
Idealistic expectations, emotions I need to
divorce
Are as difficult to tame as a wild brumby horse.
My partner is not my parent, nor a prince or
mighty earl,
I am a fully grown woman, not an immature
little girl.
My emotions are mine to handle, so
self-validation is key,
We are responsible for ourselves alone, as I'm
sure you would agree.

Shadows

Not your average companion,
Their soul is mostly dim.
You step on out into the light,
and you will let them in.
They dance and step and bend and flow,
moving to your beat.
Be them friend or enemy,
They're near impossible to defeat.
Forlorn shapes of forgotten trees,
leaves upon the ground,
Shadows come in many forms,
where light is, they can be found.
The physical shadows which float around
you in your every day,
can seldom be compared to those
which never fade away.
Shadows flitting through the mind,
popping in and out.
Others acting as blackened pits
which breed the scar of doubt.
Light shines through in certain ways,
and it patches up the wounds.
But below the pits still fester
and you feel like you're marooned.
The shadows on the inside

are jealous of those ones out.
As surface shadows have freedom,
those below go without.

Brain Fog

A day in class, my brain on mute,
Can't engage, can't compute.
I can't relax, my brain's too loud,
Inside my head is a roaring crowd.
Unsure in social situations,
I try to avoid most confrontations.
Paying attention is like a demonstration,
Struggling to keep up with conversation.
Can talk for hours about hyper fixations,
My books, fun facts and proudest creations.
A tomboy by nature, I strive to be better,
The little girl within, I loathe to upset her.
Sensitive to certain noise, indecisive by nature,
I tend to overspend and leave the consequences
till later.
I have no idea what I have, no sort of diagnosis,
I work and work to no avail, my brain is just
atrocious.

The Purple Room - Part 1

I saw the sign out front. It read: 'Room for rent. $100/w. Enquire within'. My face lit up. This is what I had been looking for; a workshop outside of my home to focus on my painting. I immediately walked through the main door. It was oddly quiet in there, like I'd walked into another world. I couldn't hear the sounds of the city outside at all. It was as if the whole building was soundproof.

A man of small stature stood at the reception desk. He smelled of old cigarettes and had deep wrinkles which made it look like his face was about to melt off. His name tag read 'Seymore'. I put on my most personable smile.

"Good morning! I am here to enquire about the room you have for rent."

Seymore slowly looked up at me. His tired expression didn't faulter.

"You're the first one to enquire about that room." He didn't utter another word after that, just looked up at me with those tired eyes. I stood there awkwardly for a moment as we just looked at one another.

"So… would I be able to see it?" I asked gently, unsure how I should reapproach the topic in question. He blinked wearily but made no intention to move. He exhaled softly. "Name?" My face reddened, suddenly realising that I had asked to view the room without even introducing myself. I flusteredly apologised and gave Seymore my name, then we shook hands. Our palms didn't touch, more of a teacup handshake, which was a bit awkward on my part, however, the elderly man seemed unfazed by it.

Old Seymore methodically scrawled my name into what looked like a very old, well-kept logbook, then turned around slowly and shuffled to a small lockbox on the table behind him. He reached into his pocket and presented a set of small keys, one of which he used to promptly unlock the lockbox. He reached inside and pulled out a rusted pair of keys. I was frankly shocked at how one could let one's keys get to such a state. Seymore turned around again and shuffled to an old elevator. He motioned me to follow. I stepped inside the lift, my feet clanging on the metal floor with each step I took. The old man reached out a gnarled hand and closed the cage door. He pressed the button to the 4th floor, and the lift slowly started to climb.

My mind buzzed with excitement. This place was a beautiful vintage, like I'd travelled back in

time as soon as I stepped through the doors, and
so cheap! Real estate is so hard to find in this
city, so this room seemed Heaven sent. I knew
that this is the studio I had yearned for, and I
hadn't even seen it yet. Before I could stop
myself, I turned to Seymore.
"I'll take it, however it is!"
He looked at me blankly, but said nothing.
Although, I could've sworn I saw a flicker of
something behind his tired eyes. Pain? Guilt?

The lift came to a shuddering halt. Seymore
pulled back the cage door and stepped out into a
long hallway. The colours were very earthy;
brown, peeling wallpaper, yellowing carpet,
several cracked sconce lights lining the walls
flickered with a dim, warm glow. The place
smelled musty and, paired with the
surroundings, it gave off a forlorn aura, as if
something terrible happened in these halls long
ago that the building had yet to come to terms
with.

I followed Seymore out of the lift and down the
hallway. We walked slowly. It almost seemed as
if the old man was trying to delay. Suddenly, one
of the doors on the left side of the hall burst
open and a man's head popped out, soon
followed by the rest of his body. He was a

funny-looking sort of fellow. Auburn hair, thick-rimmed glasses, skinny build and prominent arches in his feet. Looked around his mid-30s. Seymore and I stopped in front of the door across from him. The men didn't acknowledge each other, but the auburn-haired man stared at me, eyes wide with interest.

"You're moving into that room?"

I was confused by his question. "I don't see why not. It's just a room, is it not?"

The man's face didn't change, his eyes still wide. "No one has lived there for a few decades now", he replied.

I struggled to find something to say, but the man cut me off. "I'm Alistair. Good luck." And with that, Alistair shut his door.

"He's an odd one," old Seymore spoke up. "Never really leaves his room."

"What did he mean by "good luck"?" I questioned. Seymore only offered me a grunt in reply. They're both strange, I thought to myself. Seymore presented the rusted keys and unlocked the door. We both stepped inside. The first thing I noticed as I entered the room were the bright purple walls. It looked as if the purple Teletubby had exploded and his skin had stuck itself to the surrounding area. I winced at the intensity of the colour. It was a stark contrast to the brownness of the walls in the hallway and the reception area. They would have to be painted over immediately.

It wasn't the tidiest of rooms either. The tatty carpet was coated with a thin layer of dust, with a huge brown stain on the far-right-hand side of the room. Barely-together wooden furniture was strewn about the room in a random fashion, and miscellaneous objects had made a home for themselves in small piles at all four corners of the room. A huge window with worn lace curtains was positioned on the wall directly across from the doorway. It looked out onto the city street below. It wasn't open, but the curtains moved as if a light breeze were streaming through the room. It was quite bizarre.

"Clean up won't be necessary." I was broken out of my thoughts by the gruff voice of old Seymore.
"What do you mean?"
"Exactly that. Don't you dare touch a damn thing in this room." I looked at him, taken aback by this strange rule.
"Why ever not? It will be my room, won't it?"
"Just work around the mess. Try not to disturb the peace."

Before I could get the chance to argue, he left without another word, shoving the keys into my hands as he left. I stood in the doorway, taking in the room I've just made my new art studio. If working around the mess was the only condition of this rent, then I was happy to do it. No wonder the rent is so cheap, I thought.

I surveyed the room. The broken furniture would be easy enough to navigate around, I figured. I stepped cautiously around bits of shattered wood. It was a shame I couldn't sweep any of this up. I gingerly made my way over to the small piles in the four corners of the room. They were heavily coated in dust, but I could still tell that they were objects meant for a newborn baby. Stained, off-pink cloth nappies, a few knit baby socks, bottle teats and parts of what I can assume was a star mobile. Why would Seymore put this room up for rent? I questioned. He doesn't want anything moved, so obviously there's some form of emotional attachment he has to this room. I looked back around at the broken furniture and the dark stain on the carpet. I felt uneasy. There was some history here, a dark history that I wasn't aware of or privy to.

Just left of the large window, almost completely hidden by the curtain, I saw a wooden structure

that was unlike the rest. I walked over, careful
with my footing around the scattered objects,
and pulled back the curtain. It was a baby's cot.
At the head of the cot, laid a dusty grey stuffed
rabbit toy with cornflower blue button eyes
staring up at me. The toy itself looked normal
enough, but it felt like it had an unnatural or
otherworldly energy surrounding it.

"That belonged to Sophie", a voice whispered. I
jumped and spun around. Alistair stood behind
me, the same look on his face as before. Lost in
my exploration of the room, I must've forgotten
to close the door behind me. I was about to tell
him to bugger off out of my room, but his
comment made me pause.

"Sophie?" I asked. Alistair smiled, his eyes
sparkling. It was almost as if he were the human
embodiment of the Cheshire Cat.

"Old Seymore had a daughter. Sophie. This was
many years ago, when I was a little boy living
here with my father. She was only a few months
off a year old when she died."

I looked back at the rabbit in the cot. It looked
so… lonely. Just lying there all by itself. A
loneliness which spanned decades.

"How did she die?" I found myself asking.

"It's a mystery. The paramedics who came to the
scene chalked it up to sudden infant death
syndrome. But I think the tenants who lived here

at the time knew the real reason. The kid was smothered in her sleep by her mother."

The rabbit's button eyes pierced me, seemingly egging me on to ask more questions, to immerse myself in its history.

"Sophie's mother?"

"Yes. Madeline. She never wanted the baby to begin with. Sophie was technically an accident. Seymore loved his wife more than anything, but she was terribly neglectful to that child and he knew it. On the night young Sophie died, I remember her crying for hours on end, and then it suddenly just stopped. The next day, the paramedics were here trying to revive a baby that was already stone cold and white as a sheet. Everyone already knew what had happened, even Seymore, although he didn't want to believe it at first. A short while after the incident, Madeline just disappeared. We never saw her again. No one bothered to question it, she'd probably just run away out of guilt for what she had done. Seymore was a changed man after that. Never quite healed from that part of his life."

Alistair went quiet. I broke my gaze away from the rabbit and looked up at him. He was staring down at the rabbit too; his eyes had taken on a sadness.

"Poor little thing", he muttered. Then, he turned
and went to walk out the door, but paused, not
bothering to look back.
"If you ask me, I reckon Seymore knows more
about his wife's disappearance than he lets on."
With that, Alistair left the room. I stood
watching the doorway for an uncounted amount
of time. So that was it; that was the history of
this room which old Seymore had not allowed
me to be privy to. I shuddered and replaced the
curtain. Putting the cot and the rabbit out of
sight and out of mind would be the best thing to
do if I wanted to get any real work done. The
story may even prove to be some sort of twisted
inspiration for my art, I mused.

Over the next few days, I started slowly moving
in my art supplies. I gradually got used to
moving around the mess of the room, almost like
second nature. The chaos of the room even
seemed to add to the whole art studio ambiance.
I didn't see Alistair very much, he seemed to
keep mostly to himself. As did Seymore. Every
time I brought in a new addition to my studio
and saw him at the front desk, he would turn
away, as if he couldn't bear to look at me taking
new furniture up into that room. I knew I
shouldn't be bothered. His daughter died in that
room. I chose not to bring it up.

On the third day, I opted to stay in the apartment overnight. That way, I could get everything settled and get more used to the new space where I would be spending most of my time. The next day, I would collect my easel and my studio would be complete. I set up a sleeping bag amidst the mess. The lights in the room didn't seem to work, so I lit a few candles which my mother had given to me. They were red rose scented, so they made the room smell heavenly. It was raining that night, so I made sure that the window was shut and that there were no leaks; it was an old building after all. After I had deemed the place leak free, I set an alarm on my phone for six o'clock and resigned myself to sleep. It was in the early hours of the morning when I found myself tossing and turning in my sleep. My dreams felt like they were happening in real time and they were reoccurring, like a broken record on repeat. In the dream, a woman in a satin black nightgown paced the room. In the cot by the window, I heard a baby crying. The woman covered her eyes with her palms, digging her nails into her scalp.

"Shut up," she whispered. "Shut up, shut up, shut up, shut up, SHUT UP!" she finally screamed, turning toward the cot. She slowly moved toward it, the baby still crying wildly. I

stood up and walked over so that I could get a
better view of the baby in the cot, but the woman
stepped into my line of sight, blocking my view.
She reached her arms out to pick up the child, as
if in a trance. Instead of grabbing the child,
however, she took the pillow situated beside the
baby in the cot and lifted it over the baby's head.
I lurched forward. This woman can't be doing
what I think she's doing, can she? My arm
reached out to grab her shoulder as she lowered
the pillow on top of the crying baby's face, only
to find that my arm… went right through her. I
stood there, staring at the scene before me. I
reached out again, trying to grab the woman's
hair this time, but it was no use. The display
before me was completely out of my grasp. As I
struggled to get a grip of this woman, I heard the
baby's smothered cries dampen, until silence
descended upon the room. The woman let out a
sound which sounded like a sob, but it happened
again, and again. That's when I realise that the
woman wasn't sobbing at all; she was laughing.
Her manic laughter consumed the small room.
Then, she turned around. The woman's pupils
were so blown up, it made her eyes look black.
She stared at me as if she could see me, her
manic smile still plastered on her face.
Somehow, in that moment, a name came to me.

"Madeline", I croaked out. Her smile widened, if that were even possible. Then, she lunged at my throat.

My eyes shot open. I was coated in a layer of cold sweat. My chest and back felt clammy as my wet clothes clung to my torso. A foul smell had engulfed the room, which was odd as I had been burning the candles not long before I fell asleep. I tried to sit up, but it felt as if the sleeping bag had shrunk around me, pinning me to the ground. The rain was pouring down hard outside, and a bolt of lightning made the room light up momentarily. It was only then that I noticed the pair of black, bulging eyes looking down on me. The same woman from the dream, Madeline, was sitting on my chest, restraining me. I tried to scream, but nothing came out. I felt trapped. My body squirmed under the weight, at least trying to get an arm loose, but escape was futile. Madeline looked down on me, that same insane smile on her face. This time, however, her teeth were a filthy brown. Her black nightgown was torn and peeling, a stark contrast from her white, luminescent skin. Her head was bloated, as if in the first stage of decomposition, and tilted at such an angle that I saw the dark bruises that covered her neck. Madeline parted her swollen lips, her jaw unhinging like a snake. Her neck snapped as the rest of her body spun around, her head remaining in place, staring at me, mouth agape. I was helpless to do anything except stare in fear as she began to use all four of her limbs to move herself off my chest and toward the far wall. The whole time she kept eye contact with me, slowly manoeuvring herself, bones cracking and crunching as she moved. Only as she got further away did I dare to blink. The woman, or what I assumed was formerly a woman, was gone. It was only then that I realised she had disappeared right where the brown stain on the carpet met with the wall. I didn't sleep for the rest of the night.

The next morning, I decided that the whole experience was the result of a nightmare, and perhaps too much caffeine throughout the day. After a hot cup of peppermint tea to calm my nerves, I set out to collect my easel.

Once my easel was set up, I was ready to begin my work. I set up the canvas, got my paints ready and took a moment. When it came time to finally put my brush to canvas, I started to paint. Slowly, an image started to form. I was so lost in my work, it felt as if I was in a trance as I painted. My brush kept going back to the paint, choosing colours and applying them to the canvas as if my hand was being guided by someone else, as crazy as that sounds. When I came out of the trance, deeming it finished, I stepped back from my work to assess it. To my surprise, I had painted a baby. It was honestly better than any of my previous works. The painting was almost lifelike. The child was obviously female, with the way the pale pink cloth nappy fitted her. Her skin was pale, almost white, and her lips were a light shade of blue. Odd, I thought. Maybe I was going for a more surrealist look? The baby looked to be soundly sleeping, eyes closed and at peace. I gazed upon her face. It was so beautiful. Apart from the skin, the child-like innocence was captured perfectly. I then looked at the other figure in the painting, and that's when my blood ran cold. In the baby's arms, was a grey rabbit with cornflower blue buttons for eyes. It stared back at me. A chilling feeling overtook me. I let out a dry heave. I was unexpectedly overcome with a grief so strong I felt physically sick. My breathing became shallow and I suddenly felt as if I were drowning. My chest felt tight. I ran to the window and threw it open. My breaths were deep and shuddering. I sucked in air as if my life depended on it. Tears ran down my cheeks and clouded my vision. When I felt my breath start to come and go in a steady fashion, I turned around and sat on the window ledge, composing myself. First a nightmare-ridden night and now shortness of breath? I figured that I would ask Seymore later on if there was any existing asbestos in the insulation.

A small bump came from the cot side of the room, bringing me out of my thoughts. I quickly glanced over. Through the blur of the unshed tears in my eyes, I noticed a small shape moving around in the cot behind the curtain. The breeze from the open window lightly blew the curtain to the side to offer me a glimpse at what the shape was. My breath caught in my throat. Standing at the edge of the cot, staring right at me, was the rabbit with the cornflower blue button eyes. It started at me, but I couldn't sense any malice coming from it. Instead, it tilted its small head, its long ears flopping to one side. I wanted to run. This was insane. Had I been breathing in too many paint fumes? It didn't matter anyway. I went to move only to find myself frozen in place. I was at this thing's mercy. Slowly, it reached out both its arms towards me, as if it wanted me to pick it up. Then, just as suddenly as it started, the rabbit dropped back into the cot, inanimate once again.

I let out a slow, shuddering breath. I hadn't realised that I had been holding it the whole time. What just happened? Had I imagined it? Was it a trick of my mind? Maybe it was my unease with the knowledge of the history of this room that had me on edge. Perhaps it was due to not enough sleep. I tried to shake it off. This wasn't productive for my work. I needed to clear my head if I was to continue my art in a manner of my satisfaction. I decided to go for a walk. I grabbed my satchel from beside my easel and walked out the door, leaving the painting and creepy stuffed animal in the cot behind. As I strode out of the building, old Seymore watched me go. He didn't have his usual blank expression though. Instead, he looked at me warningly, as if to say "forget about what you saw". I pursed my lips in an awkward smile and quickly stepped out into the bustling city.

The Purple Room - Part 2

The walk home was refreshing. It felt good to be out amongst the lively public. With my newly clear head, I chalked up my experience in the room to being a fantastical figment of my imagination. It was a simple case of me hearing a story and it having a profound impact on me, along with a terrible sleep. That was all. It was actually just what I needed for my art, as much as it made me uneasy. I had seemingly found a medium, and I was going to use it as my inspiration until my creative well had dried up. I turned the corner and walked back up the street to the old building.

As I approached it, I noticed that one of the rooms had its window open, letting the curtains loose in the breeze outside. It was then I realised that the room in question was my own. I had forgotten to close the window! Registering that there was the possibility of leaves and debris currently flying around the room and all over my still-wet painting, I chastised myself and quickened my pace, the soles of my shoes slapping on the sidewalk. Finally, I got to the entrance of the building. As I reached for the handle, I noticed some movement coming from my window in the corner of my eye. My head shot up, and I immediately turned white as a sheet. The head of the stuffed rabbit was peering over the window sill down at me, its bright blue button eyes fixed on me. Suddenly, a gnarled hand reached over and grabbed its ears. The hand was pallid and the nails were long. It was the hand of a woman. Just as abruptly as the hand had shown itself, it pulled the rabbit by its ears back inside. I gasped. Someone was in my room. I gripped the handle to the entrance and threw open the door. I ran inside and towards the lift as fast as I could. Before I could reach for the cage, a hand gripped my wrist. My eyes snapped up to meet old Seymore's. He glared at me.

"Don't go up there." His voice sounded lighter, fearful. I stared back at him for a moment and he loosened his grip.

"Please," Seymore begged. "You can't go up there."

I exhaled softly. "Who's up there?"

"Her."

I immediately thought of the horrific figure I thought I imagined the night before. Madeline. I started to feel anger bubble up inside me, common sense tearing me out of my

irrationality. I ripped my arm out of his grasp
and flung open the cage to the lift.

"I don't care!" I yelled. "Somebody is
trespassing in my apartment!"

I saw a look of resignation cross Seymore's face,
which then turned to determination.

"Then I'll go with you." He said simply. With
that, we both stepped into the lift and made our
way up to the 4th floor.

I practically sprinted down the hallway,
fumbling with my rusted keys. Seymore
followed close behind. He was surprisingly fast
for his age. I shoved a key into the lock and
forced the door open to find… nothing. The
window was open, to be sure, and the curtains
fluttered around chaotically with the breeze.
Even though the city was right outside, the room
was silent. I cautiously stepped into the room.
"Hello?" I called. Nothing. Seymore poked his
head around the doorframe. I ignored him,
studying the room. Whoever had been here had
barely touched a thing. I looked around for the
stuffed rabbit, only to find it sitting upright
against the wall, right on top of the brown stain
on the carpet. However, that's not the thing that
sent chills up my spine. In the centre of the
room, where my easel stood, were three long
claw marks through the canvas; right across the

neck of the child I had painted. I heard old
Seymore let out a half sob.
"That painting," he began. "That looks just like
my Sophie when I found her."
I immediately knew what he meant. No wonder
the skin was so pallid and the lips blue. It was a
picture of his daughter when he found her dead
body. My blood ran cold. I looked back at
Seymore. Tears were streaming down his face as
he gazed upon the ruined canvas.
"How could you create this? How could you
possibly have known?"
Before I could tell him that I had no idea how
the image came to me, I heard a laugh. It was
soft at first, so soft that I almost mistook it for a
sob. But then it got louder, louder. The laugh
reached a pitch and a volume that Seymore and
myself had to cover our ears and hastily exit the
room. We kept retreating until we got to the end
of the hallway. Seymore looked haunted. "I
knew that room was not to be inhabited. I was a
fool for thinking I could finally put all this
behind me. I'll give you a full refund."

"Is there asbestos in the walls?" I found myself
bluntly blurting out. Seymore looked confused.
"Excuse me?"
"Asbestos" I repeated. Seymore looked at me as
if I had a screw loose.

"I don't understand what that has to do with you moving out."

I kept my gaze on him, resolute. "Oh, I'm not going anywhere. If there is any in the walls then I would like to request that we remove it as I will be spending lots of time in that room and I feel that it is already starting to affect my health and mind. Perhaps yours as well, if I may be so bold."

Seymore's mouth was agape at this point. His expression read pure disbelief. "You're mad! Did you just forget what just happened?"

I shrugged. "Hey, I suggest we give it a try. I'll even offer to chip in for the removal if it's…"

"I don't think you truly grasp the direness of the situation here!" Seymore snapped. I had never heard such heat in his voice before. "I have never met someone who has seen so many horrors before with their own eyes and still turns a blind eye. For your information, I had the asbestos removed from the walls in this room prior to the birth of my late daughter, God rest her soul. If you insist on staying here despite that, then fine, but I still strongly urge you to move out as soon as possible."

The next few days were largely uneventful. Whenever I would pass the front desk and give old Seymore a smile, he would turn away or

give me a grunt. He was probably still fuming
from the encounter we had the other day
regarding the asbestos, or lack-of-there-of. I
chose not to give it any mind. He'd get over it
sooner or later.

It was a particularly cold afternoon, so I decided
to use my portable heater to warm up the room
while I painted. The small electric outlet was
located on the side of the room near the dark
patch in the carpet. The outlet was filthy with a
brown crust in its crevices. I plugged in the
heater. The small device started up with a
shudder, and before long, the room was a
comfortable temperature to work in. I
immediately got to work setting up my paints
and my workstation.

I painted until the sun set and didn't even notice
until the room got too dark to work in. With a
sigh, I finally took my brush away from the
canvas to flick on a light. When I turned back,
something made me pause. The heater in the
corner was expelling some sort of dark
substance. I rushed over to investigate, thinking
that it might be some sort of oil that could stain
the carpet even more; one more thing to pay for.
Whatever the substance was, it was wet, sticky
and dripping from the heater, creating a small

puddle around it. I unplugged the cord, but the heater still continued to drip the dark fluid. Dipping my finger into the puddle, I brought the digit up to my nose. It smelled coppery. Like blood. A shiver ran up my spine. I swivelled around, and came face to face with the stuffed rabbit. It was standing up by itself, inches away from where I knelt. My breath caught in my throat as the toy slowly took a step towards me, reaching its arms out. I sat still, frozen, as the toy advanced, its movements were like that of a robot; stiff, unnatural. Before I could get a chance to react, the toy let out a piercing squeal, like a baby would make. That seemed to be the thing that broke me from my trance. I covered my ears and shuffled back until I was against the wall.

The large window flew open and an almighty gust of cold wind blew through, throwing back the curtains along with the toy, which flew into the opposite wall...A loud scream rang out as it went, almost deafening me, and then all went silent. It was cold, dark, still and I was terrified. I kept my eyes pinned to the rabbit against the wall. Apparently, I was directing my attention at the wrong thing. In my peripherals, I caught sight of a figure standing behind the curtains. I wanted to ask who it was, but in my heart, I already knew. For once in my life, I kept my mouth shut. The figure stepped out from behind the curtain, black dress flowing in a non-existent breeze. Madeline stepped towards the rabbit, as if stalking it like a predator. The rabbit remained still and inanimate. Madeline's mouth stretched into a twisted grin. She looked just like she did on the first night I spent in the apartment: bloated features, filthy teeth, black bulging eyes. With her careful footsteps towards the small toy came that awful cracking sound with each movement of her joints.

No, this had to be another nightmare. I must've been indulging in my painting for too long, I thought that I must be delusional. But then, how could that thing in front of me have felt so real? I couldn't stay there any longer to think, I had to get out. Going against my better judgement, I sprang up from my spot and made a mad dash towards the door. As I reached for the handle, it seemingly opened by itself. My head banged against it as it flew open. I stumbled back, cradling my head, and looked up to see old Seymore standing at the door. His eyes had taken on a steely nature, a stark contrast from their usual tiredness, and were trained on the figure behind me. I glanced back to see Madeline's manic grin turn into a grimace as she locked eyes with the old man. Seymore rigidly moved forward into the room, which made Madeline take a step back, and then another. As quick as lightning, she turned and retreated into the wall closest to the brown stain, screaming bloody murder as she went.

The room went silent again as we processed what had just happened. Finally, Seymore let out a long breath. He made his way over to the stuffed rabbit, picking it up and stroking its ears back. He took a moment, and then looked up at me. His eyes had a faraway look in them.
"I painted this room in the winter of 1980," he said softly. "Madeline never wanted the baby to begin with, but I was the one who convinced her to keep it." Seymore trained his eyes on the ground. I could tell he was holding back tears, but he had to get this story off his chest. With a dry swallow, he continued. "That morning, I found Madeline in Sophie's room, hunched into a ball and crying beside the baby's cot. I asked her what happened and quickly rushed to check on Sophie, but it was too late. My daughter looked just like you painted her. My poor baby… When I asked Madeline why she didn't call the ambulance. She didn't say a damn word." Seymore took a moment to gather his thoughts enough to continue. "Paramedics came,

but they couldn't do anything for my baby girl.
They said it was sudden infant death syndrome.
When they came out with the cause of death I
looked to Madeline for comfort, but she was
stoic. I even thought that I saw the corners of her
mouth twitch. That was when I knew that
Sophie's death was no accident. It was days later
that I finally got up the courage to ask Madeline
what had really happened to our baby. She got
this little smirk on her face and said that we
didn't have to worry about it anymore. That she
took care of it. That we could finally go back to
how we used to be". He snarled. I felt his rage
from here. How couldn't I? This man had held
onto this grief for years and had never come to
terms with it. I looked around the room at the
broken furniture. Seymore must've noticed
because he quickly went on with the story.

"I was so mad that I started breaking things. It
was as if a demon had possessed me. Every bit
of furniture that I had built for my baby, all
useless now. Madeline grabbed my arms and
tried to stop me, saying that she'd done it for us,
for our future. I couldn't even stand to look at
her. In my blind rage, I grabbed her by the neck
and squeezed. She was the reason why I could
no longer hold my baby, caress her, whisper that
I loved her. Madeline was the reason why I was

feeling a grief so intense that I felt like I was
going to die from it. I kept squeezing and
squeezing until there was no breath left in her
body, and even that wasn't enough. I grabbed the
first thing I could reach, a broken chair leg, and
started stabbing her body. My vision was blurry
and I felt the tears running down my face but, in
that moment, I no longer loved that woman. She
was the devil in my eyes. And I suppose she
became an embodiment of that in the end" he
added, breaking out of his trance to look around
the purple room.

I looked over to the brown stain on the carpet
and gulped, my mouth suddenly feeling dry.
"What did you do with the body?"
"I put it in the back of my truck, rolled up in a
carpet, and drove outside the city limits. I kept
driving and driving. It felt like I was in a trance.
Then, when I felt I was far enough, I dumped
her body in a ravine. As far as I know, her body
was never discovered. Police never came
knocking. I don't regret what I did" Seymore
said coldly. "She had it coming from the
moment the thought entered her mind to harm
my child. I was only doing what any father
would."
"That's not true," I said. "Yes, anybody with a
child would want to protect them and seek

vengeance for their death, but acting upon it and merely thinking it are two different things. Doesn't it weigh on your conscience that you killed your wife?"

"Every. Damn. Day" He gritted through his teeth. "Even though I don't regret killing my baby's murderer, I feel empty without my family. My life has felt like it has no purpose…" He suddenly got quiet, as if a thought had only just occurred to him. Then, slowly, old Seymore started walking towards the open window. When he got to the ledge, he turned his head back to face me.

"I haven't told a single soul the truth about that night until now." He paused for a moment. "You want these horrors to stop, right?" I nodded. Seymore gave me a sad smile. "Then I think I know how. I know Madeline. Even in death, she's a petty bitch." He looked me directly in the eye and gave me a smile. "Be sure to paint over those walls for me. I never liked that shade of purple."

With that, he let go, falling forward out of the open window and into the cold night air below. I tried to scream, but all that came out was a whisper. Nothing but the hard thud of a body hitting the pavement met me in reply. Then, as if by some miracle, the room stilled. The whole atmosphere somehow felt… lighter.

Abiding by Seymore's last wish, I painted over the walls. I decided on white, as it just felt like the room could use a fresh start after all these years. I even volunteered to arrange Seymore's funeral, as I discovered that he had no other living relatives. It was quite sad really. I didn't think that his death would affect me as much as it did.

True to old Seymore's word, the strange happenings in the formerly-purple room stopped. Even though this was the case, I still felt that the room harboured too many memories and too much past trauma to even think of remaining as a resident in it. I moved out of the room two weeks later. Yet, even though all of this happened many years ago, I am still haunted by visions. Every time I close my eyes, a vivid memory hits me. I still see Seymore's body falling from that open window, but this time, a woman in black, holding a baby, follows after him in his descent to death.

Average Joe

Being praised all the time while growing up as a child isn't always a good thing. Joe grew up believing that he was one in a million, a talent which only came once in a lifetime, that it was his world and others just lived in it. Knitting, sewing, public speaking, drawing. Even mundane tasks around the house. Joe was praised extensively for many things which most children would simply get a "good job" for. He got trophies in competitions, awards and recognition for his creativity from outside sources. Growing up in a small town, where only a minority were creatively-minded, it did not come as a shock to Joe that he was gaining recognition within this close-minded community. Imagine the blow when he left home and got out into the world and found that others also have unique talents of their own; talents which Joe did not possess. Joe soon realised that he was a simple case of knowing to do a lot of things, yet he could only do them at an average level. This led to an almost debilitating case of people-pleasing, just so that he could get praised again like he did as a child. Everything Joe did, which he used to get rewarded for, he felt wasn't good enough. He had reached a level of perfectionism where he felt he had to control everything around him in order to get his desired outcome. This went on for several years. It has only been recently that Joe realised that doing things at an average level isn't a terrible thing. He knows how to do tons of things. At least he's not horrible at them. Average is halfway up the scale of good and awful, and, if Joe hones his skills further, there's still the chance to become brilliant at certain things. For now, Joe is content to be an Average Joe. But Average Joe will always have room to grow.

My Flatmate is a Vampire

"And here's the key, Noah. I hope that you settle in well."

"Thanks, Mrs R, I'm sure I will."

"Now, remember the rules. No friends over after 9 pm."

Noah smiled. "There's absolutely no need for worry there, Mrs R." After being discharged from the army after his deployment for medical reasons, Noah became a bit of a loner. He was hoping that a fresh start in a new apartment would help him move on from his past. He was secretly quite lonely, and Mrs Rhodes knew it. The elderly landlady gave him a sad smile. "Just remember that you're always welcome to pop round to my room for a cuppa."

"Much appreciated, I'll let you know".

With that, Noah Davies was now part owner of an apartment on the busiest street in Bristol, along with a mysterious renter whom Noah safely assumed didn't live on the premises.

After unpacking, Noah indulged himself in a cup of hot tea and sat on a seemingly well-used chair that was situated by the small old-fashioned telly in the living room. As he sipped his tea, he thought about how homely this apartment seemed, yet, Noah swore that he could feel a set of eyes watching him as he unpacked his old army gear and hung up his clothes. It was an old living space and looked like it hadn't been used for years, although this chair and some of the other furniture showed indications that someone had lived there recently. The mysterious renter that was supposed to be his roommate? But that was impossible, he thought. Mrs Rhodes had told him that the previous owner was a man who had died decades ago. He'd been found in a park a day after he was reported missing, stabbed twelve times in the abdomen and buried in a shallow grave. This is where he was found by a council worker on their way to work in the early hours of a morning in March 1952. Two months later, the murderer was caught (via information from an anonymous source), the man was buried properly and everyone went on with their lives. But, mysteriously, the rent for the apartment kept being paid monthly, as per usual, and Mrs Rhodes had no choice but to accept it. It has been this way for years now, so Noah felt that he was safe to assume that he was the apartment's only occupant. With the addition of half the rent being paid for by a complete stranger.

Noah supposed that his tea needed some more milk, and hoped that Mrs R had stocked the fridge before his arrival. He moved through the space, sometimes sucking in his stomach to squeeze between pieces of furniture, which seemed to be clustered all over the place. When he finally entered the kitchen, after the arduous task of dodging and weaving through the living room, the strong, tangy aroma of copper struck his nose at once. It reminded him immediately of his army days, and he felt himself begin to twitch with the bloody reminder. Death was not something that bothered Noah, not in the least. He had seen enough of it during his deployment to last his entire lifetime.

As he neared the fridge, the smell seemed to get increasingly stronger and stronger, until he was forced to cover his nose with the front of his shirt. Without hesitation, he forced open the door of the fridge only to come face to face with what looked like a scene from a slasher film. Blood covered the walls of the fridge and was hardened to a dry crust that caked the walls and looked as if it wouldn't come off without putting up a fight. Even though panic and confusion clouded Noah's thoughts, he still made a mental note to buy some heavy-duty cleaning product and a tough sponge. Bags of blood lined the shelves

and severed body parts were jammed into the
crisper at the bottom of the fridge. Noah took a
step back in shock, only to collide with
something hard.

He spun around and met the furious eyes of a
pale man with sharp facial features and messy
blonde curls atop his head that stuck out in all
directions. At first glance, he looked to be in his
late twenties, but the dark circles under his eyes
suggested that he was wiser than his looks made
him seem. The man smelt just as bad as the
fridge, and Noah picked up the scent of death
and formaldehyde seeping out of his pores.
Noah stood stock still, unsure of what to do.

"W-Who a-are you?" he managed to stammer
out. The man tilted his head to the side and gave
Noah a cold look that made the very blood in his
veins freeze.
They stood like that for a while, before Noah
finally got up the sliver of confidence he needed
to probe this man further. He was a soldier after
all; there was no time to crumple from fear in
the face of a potential enemy.
"What are you doing in my apartment?" he
asked, straightening his spine and looking the
tall man dead in the eyes. He could feel the
man's frigid breath on his face. They were

standing so close. It was making Noah feel slightly uncomfortable, and being under the stranger's penetrating gaze made Noah like a bug under a microscope. He hated this feeling. Before he could react further, the man spoke with a thick northern Irish accent.

"I'm afraid you are mistaken, Noah. This is *my* apartment. It has been for the last fifty years. Give or take a few." The strange studied him further, keeping his icy glare steady as he took in Noah's appearance.

"What rank?"

"What?"

"You heard me. I will not repeat myself."

"Oh… um… Warrant Officer. How…?"

"The way you present yourself. I've seen it all before. I lived through the second world war, after all. I'm guessing you got discharged with PTSD? I assume that's what they're calling it these days. In my day we'd call it shell shock and lock a man up…"

"I'm sorry to interrupt, but who are you? And how do you know my name?" Noah's sudden interruption earned him a glare from the pale stranger, before he turned and stalked into the living room. Noah followed close on his heels, desperate for information. The man sat down on the chair that Noah formerly resided in and directed his eyes on the veteran, thin hands steepled under his chin.

"I can see that you're confused," the man started. "I suppose that since you're now paying for half the rent now owe you an explanation. My name is Callum O' Ryan. I became accustomed with *your* name from the dogtags in the front pocket of your duffel bag." The man pulled the aforementioned dog tags out of his jacket pocket and held them in a pale, bony hand out to Noah, who snatched them off the man and pocketed them, appalled at the blonde man's audacity. "This is my apartment that you now reside in," Callum continued. "o don't think that I'm making any exceptions concerning my meals now that we are roommates. Oh, speaking of which, fetch me a bag from the fridge, I'm practically dying here!" He scoffed at his little inside joke that he knew Noah wouldn't understand and waved his hand towards the veteran as an indication to complete the task he was set. Noah reluctantly fetched a blood bag from the fridge of horrors and passed it towards his 'roommate'. He frankly had no idea why he was abiding by this man's wishes, after all, the man had already invaded his private possessions, but it just seemed like the right thing to do.Callum studied the blood with a critical eye and gave Noah a quick smirk, before opening his mouth to reveal two, long, gleaming, sharp canines that descended from his gums. He made eye contact with Noah as he sunk his fangs into the blood bag and continued to drain it of its contents. When the bag was empty, he tossed it behind the sofa without a second thought. Noah stumbled back, horrified at what he just witnessed. It wasn't possible!

Callum lazily rolled his neck and arched his back, stretching the muscles that had gone so long without proper use. As he stretched, his shirt rode up over his stomach, and Noah could clearly see twelve scars (made by a butcher's knife) in the abdominal region. Noah gasped and staggered back further.
"You're the man Mrs R told me about. You're supposed to be dead! How is this possible?" Noah choked out. Callum glanced up to meet his eyes again and smiled, but this smile appeared genuine. It seemed to calm Noah down a touch and allowed Callum a moment to admire Noah's brave curiosity. No one had ever stayed this long before. Noah was equally as impressed with his willingness to stay despite the impossibilities drawn out before him. Callum was obviously some kind of monster, and yet, he hadn't

attacked Noah, or even shown any animosity towards him. He seemed safe.

"So, Mrs R told you about me, I see. Yes. My death was rather unfortunate, a 'spanner in the works' you could call it. Yet, she still lets me lead out my eternal existence here. Bless her old soul. I see why she allowed you to move in with me."

Noah looked at him questioningly. "And why is that then?"

Callum smirked. "Because you're the only one who hasn't run away screaming."

From then on, Noah and Callum lived together harmoniously in the apartment. Noah ran errands for Callum during daylight hours, and, in return, Callum offered Noah a listening ear and good company. Noah appreciated the company more than anything. Callum was rude, sarcastic and quite blunt, but Noah's patience and easy-going nature seemed to balance that out quite well. The blatant disregard for social niceties even felt comforting after a while. Callum himself even seemed to open up and take comfort in Noah's presence as the months drew on. For the first time in his life, Noah felt like he had made his first real friend.

Perspective

The first sip of hot coffee on a cold day.
Taking time out for yourself to read that book
you always said you'd read.
Cuddling on the couch with your pets.
Warm, starry nights on the veranda.
The clean feeling of freshly washed sheets.
Pink sunsets in winter, the cool breeze on your
cheeks.
Stepping into a warm shower on a warm night.
Knitting to heavy metal music.
Stepping into a cold puddle in just your socks.
The tag on the back of your shirt that always
scratches your back but you keep forgetting to
cut off.
A mosquito bite on the arch of your foot.
Realising that we are all going to die someday
and there's nothing we can do about it.
The speck of dust that is our planet in the vast
universe.
You are so small in the grand scheme of things.
You're dying every day, every second which
passes.
Your mark on this world will become
non-existent in years to come.

You are a part of the larger human population,
born only to grow, reproduce and die.
That first sip of hot coffee tastes different now,
huh?

A Moment to Reminisce

I grew up in a regional town. My backyard was fairly average, and fenced off from a larger paddock which was owned by the meatworks. I have always owned dogs. I remember a lot about my home life there; sometimes it was happy and most of the time it wasn't, so I spent a lot of my youth at my grandparents' house. Their house was my favourite place to go as a child. I memorised grandma's phone number at a very young age and whenever I was bored at home, I would always give grandma a call and ask her to come pick me up. I used to love playing in their pool, eating my weight in lollies and playing snakes and ladders with grandma. Sometimes we would even set up the toy train set and watch the train go around the tracks while we built a city around it out of coloured wooden blocks. I would also watch cartoons on the paid channels which I didn't get at home.

On weekends, before my brother was born, dad took me out to see his parents in the country regularly. It was always hot and dusty out there, but I knew that dad had work to do. Dad's parents were never particularly stimulating company, so I would just amuse myself by going walkabout through the bush (within dad's sight).

Once, I told dad that I was bored and he killed and gutted a pig in front of me. My uncle also instructed me to pluck a dead duck if I had nothing else to do. I was four years old. Never again have I consciously told my dad that I was bored. If I did hint that I was bored, dad would ask me to dig up the bindis in the yard or mow the lawn. I loathed chores, so I would always decline and go back to brooding in the monotony of my life.

I don't remember going out to the country much after the pig incident. Not a huge loss for me, as I still had my grandma and pop to offer me amusement. I used to travel with them from the time my brother was born until I was 20 years old. Grandma, Pop and I would go to the theme parks and the beach on the Gold Coast, go shopping in Brisbane, stroll around the busy city in Sydney, and look at flowers in Spring in Canberra. Particular memories which stand out include the time where I made pop pay for a $30 bag of lollies for me (which I never finished), grandma and pop laughing at me while struggling to find their camera as a homeless man's rat scurried about on my head (yes, this sounds weird with no context), and an old man at the War Memorial in Hyde Park who only my brother and I saw

Healing

Healing feels like making time for ten minutes of meditation in the rush of the everyday. Healing feels like sitting on the couch with your pets or loved ones and taking a mental snapshot in time to remember this feeling. Healing is realising the things within and outside your control and remaining content in that knowledge. Healing is knowing what is good for me and acting upon it. Healing is breaking down walls and defence mechanisms over time to those who truly deserve your true self. Healing is having support there, and realising that you will never be abandoned; that you don't have to abandon your true self in order to be accepted by others; that those who love you and all your idiosyncrasies will find you. Healing is knowing what you are willing to put up with and where the limits lie. Healing is pulling yourself out of unhealthy situations because it is no longer benefitting you. Healing can also be stepping away or not participating in conversations which you find triggering. First impressions view healing as a selfish act, but it is much more than that. Finding peace within yourself is healthy for your perception, your relationships, and your future as a human on this earth. Finding the time to heal will lead to the enhanced human experience. I believe that this is what we all deserve.